WHITE BOYS FROM HELL

JEFFREY SKINNER

C&R Press
Conscious & Responsible

Winnter Soup Bowl Chapbook
2018 5th Collection Selection 2 of 2 CB 10

Printed in the United States of America

First Edition
1 2 3 4 5 6 7 8 9

Cover Art by Max Rippon
Interior and cover design by C&R Press
Copyright ©2018 Jeffrey Skinner

ISBN-13: 978-1-936196-97-5

C&R Press
Conscious & Responsible
www.crpress.org

For special discounted bulk purchases, please contact:
C&R Press sales@crpress.org
Contact info@crpress.org to book events, readings and author signings.

WHITE BOYS FROM HELL

For Tom Byers

ACKNOWLEDGEMENTS

Disclaimer Magazine (UK): "The Channel Swimmer"

Ploughshares: "For My Brother Who Couldn't Stay"

The Los Angeles Review: "Insomnia" and "The Nighthawk"

Manhattan Review: "Locality"

Michigan Quarterly Review: "Shush" and "The Truth About Men"

New England Review: "Tips for Zazen, with Acknowledgment of Certain Eschatological Concerns" and "Love & Judgment"

TABLE OF CONTENTS

Shush

The women are calling out the men
& rightly so. I'm over here trying not to make noise.
I'm poor, the only sins I can afford
Are handmade. Mostly I watch TV. There, it's sex
& death—dawn to dusk. It's 3D desire in Dolby Atmos.
But, where is it not? I want
To climb in, into the confetti mass
Of electrons, to ululate among those golden mean
Faces, maybe snap one off like a virtual flower.

But mama said, *You dasn't, you dasn't,*
An imperative so whispery, so soft in the mouth
It almost seems unsounded, telepathic.
Mama's like everyone now—
In a home, she doesn't know where.
The saline bag's been needled, she's leaking out.

Anyway, it wasn't mama who said *dasn't*—
That was my German grandmother
Who died early, in a time when the terminal weren't told.
I lug the OED to the mahogany high desk & look—
Yep, the definition of mercy has changed.

But I remember seeing her before I went to college.
She knew, it was in her eyes. I knew she knew.

The Truth About Men

I was around seven when mother found my drawing of a naked woman. Although I was hazy about female anatomy, I had recently surprised her as she came out of the shower. I deliberately made the drawing more baroque than necessary, adding lines and flourishes, especially to the breasts and pubis, which had become a mass of heavily inked black commas. My mother sat me down and placed the drawing before me on the kitchen table. "This is interesting," she said. "What is it a picture of?" "A machine," I answered. "Hmmm . . . it looks like a woman to me," she said, "a woman without her clothes. Is that it?" "No." She smiled at me and placed her hand on my head, then gently stroked my cheek. "It's all right if you've made a picture of a woman without her clothes," she said. "Is that what this is, a naked woman?" I looked away, out the kitchen window, at the weeping willow in our front yard. If you clipped a branch at just the right place and then stripped it of leaves it made an excellent whip. "It's ok. You can tell me." "No," I answered, knowing I would lie as many times as I was asked. "It's a machine."

Free Will

When I consider the idea of space as notebooks
We fill with words, I immediately think: No, there
Aren't enough words—the field shifts so rapidly
Even if we wrote like furious monkeys
We could not account for a single morning.
So I searched for another substance, one
That might rise from three or more dimensions
To take on the breath & volition of, say, dew
On a blade of grass. Which I could drink. And drink.
But then everything I touched became illusion—
I had the *maya* touch, a joke everyone got, & moved
Away from me. After I slept that off, I rose
& found the world more or less as I left it.
But I was changed. I still imagine my eyes create
Trees outside my window, which I am free
To call *Jeff Trees*. Also: *Jeff Dogs, Jeff Children, Jeff
Awards*, etc. Without my seeing, this version
Would be lost. Will be lost. I'm not the substance,
I'm not the notebook. I'm not even these words.
But I can, if I want, imagine I'm god. It is permitted.

Sometimes I Am the Fantastic Weight Beneath My Own Saddle

Did you hear what the rebels did
Dragged a woman naked to the town square

Raped her hacked her to death
Because she put pieces

Of local fish into the beans & thereby spoiled
Their protection spell

But that is the very thing *I* wanted to do
When I was my own horse

Led by desire—
Lord, we learn nothing, only go outside

When the music of narcosis leaks from clouds
Then only to lick

Sadness away
From each other's faces

Sometimes I am the fantastic weight
Beneath my own saddle

The nightmare horse
Who feeds on flesh not hay

Olive & Bluto & Popeye

Popeye had a good heart & could kick ass. Olive was his gal, but Bluto kept trying to steal her away. It wasn't his fault entirely: she was tempted by Bluto's huge muscles & deep voice. But he was a cad, out only for himself. In fact, the actor who portrayed Bluto was a decent man, with a large, nice family, while the actor who played Popeye was a dick. We may mark this as the moment irony began to blur the line between image & truth. Nothing is known of the real woman behind Olive. However, in the abstract of a recent scholarly article by Lena Gunnarsson the author concludes: "Contrary to many contemporary feminist theorists, I contend that, although the category 'women' does not reflect the whole reality of concrete & particular women, it nevertheless refers to something real, namely the structural position as woman." I watched hundreds of hours of Popeye cartoons, loving Popeye & hating Bluto. I was neutral on Olive, though I thought it odd that both men found her hot. Today I see that no member of that ménage a trois was any great prize, & none of them could qualify as a contemporary celebrity. Here I should add that I lied about the actors who played Popeye & Bluto—I know as little about them as I do about the actress who played Olive. All I know for sure is that she was something real, a woman.

The Nighthawk

I go back to warn the guy I used to be.   But when I get there he
looks tired, eating alone in the diner. He's just come from the
four-to-twelve shift. I can't bring myself to touch his arm, or
speak. Besides, it's clear I'm not much of anything to him—a
spot of ketchup on his tie, a shadow passing through the parking
lot. He chews, looking straight ahead, beer in hand, cigarettes
and zippo on the formica counter.   And still so much night left
to go.

For My Brother Who Couldn't Stay

In this poem someone has taken the edge
of one hand & swept the crumbs
from the counter.
In this poem we save
what falls & Jesus speaks lightly,
a breeze carrying the river's scent.
And all the day & night of this poem
a face asks what's left
after science, after the black & white
movies, the forties camel hair coat, the nothing underneath.
The face in this poem asks & asks, and keeps
asking, until *Shut up,* you want to say,
I'm sick of you & your
permanent tears . . .
This poem looks out a cloudy porthole
at a branch-shaking tulip tree
scratching to be let in.
And though this poem is a good swimmer
it can never be sure of reaching the equator, let alone
the dead-center self. Maybe,
if it could play the accordion in French,
after the war, that kind of sadness . . .
But this poem would rather be the wound than play it,
would in fact widen the wound
so that we might take a deep breath & dolphin in
to the cooling blood, the salt river.
Lastly, this poem would like a word with you, Mother.
The word is: *fallopian.*
This poem, this difficulty with words—Mother, can you feel
the child beneath, breathing water?

Locality

Memory gives the lie to it,
      Bringing the far & thoroughly dissolved
            Close, the gone scene buzzing back into focus.

Here I stroke a silly beard & look away, &
      My twin does likewise, however far off in time.
            But who's that walking next to him

On the way to the toy store, tall solicitous shadow?
      Many atoms are missing from the scene
            Though enough remain to spot

The boy staring into a glass case, a Matchbox city
      Of cars, trucks & vans, boy all atwitch & wanting.
            Which has not changed. Physicists

Can so far teleport one weightless photon across a lab,
      Though distances are scheduled to increase.
            As to the boy, the once & future

Son of Hamburg, New York, Lost Boy King
      Of Thousand-Eyed Desire—that's my enormous hand
            Curved round his wet, still folded wings.

Insomnia

Walking the Möbius strip, sleep just up ahead, on the other
side. I have a strong sense of self, which I lose track of easily and
often. The dark gets all up in my face. I can see a little through
my daughter, but most of the future's socked in by fog. Thoughts
slide out before I can write them down. I'll have them in the next
world, & some will still be stupid. If salvation depended on the
social life I'd be damned. My mother keeps asking to go home,
but when I ask *which home* she can't say—not where it is, or was,
or when. At some point, wide–eyed, everyone whispers, *OK,
death, show me what you got.*

Tips for Zazen, With Acknowledgment of Certain
Eschatological Concerns

First, it's important to put the mind
In the hollow of your left palm,
Or better yet where hand meets belly
Three inches below the button;
Or, even better, that spot but further
In: inside the body itself.
The best signal is vertical so hold
The spine erect, like an antenna. If you need
A chair, be a human growing
From the chair. Yes: after long low pressure
Comes cumulus, & hard focus blue,
A certain feeling the skull breathes again.
At this point you may notice
A soothing breeze: time to double down.
And it's probable the screen
Spatters quick-cut scenes from the past,
Lacking context & thick
With unaccountable emotion. Don't
Linger; delta waves loom on the horizon.
The welcome moment may come
You feel amnesic, as if you've just returned
From some borderless silence
The will can't conjure. If so, it means
You have in fact been away
But are that very instant back, a dim
Sweetness on your tongue. Resume,
Return to counting breaths. Some days
Bring more Maya, less freedom;
Others the reverse. Let both alone. Proceed.
Pilgrim, if you think any of this
Profits your awareness, or meaning—well: it may.

Still, meaning enters every life
Noticed or not, & what's up ahead
In any case stays cloudy, just out of reach.

Love & Judgment

Of course it was October I think maybe evening at least
That's when most things happened suddenly inside me
Happened on the skeleton of a bird at forest's edge
A crispy light in & around the scrubbed-clean matchstick bones
White now as god's teeth, & as necessary, weightless

Nearly between thumb & index finger picking up the skull
A deep look my eyes so focused & sharp in those days
& the ant crawled out in tiny panic from eye socket
Onto my finger I dropped the skull though it hardly made
Any difference in hand's weight flung up ant flying off

Continued with purpose: forget the girl, what girl no matter
Walk through abandoned graveyard names all chewed
By time unreadable stone the smell of lake water
Floating just beyond opaque tannic black from surface
Down to mush black mud took off shoes walked out

A bit numb girl's face on surface broken on the way back
Picked up skull again blew hard through eyehole until clean
Dropped in shirt pocket light as origamied rolling paper
Remembered thinking skull white, & *necessary*
As god's teeth . . . Why *necessary*? Carried the question

From forest & memory of some girl almost
Loved, but what was love & judgment against nineteen years old
Everything weightless as a sparrow skull in pocket
Bobbing as I jogged through autumn the barred owls calling out
What do you know what do you know what do you know

Summer Apparition

There's something waving behind
The screen. Yes. But we can't make it out.
Scrub metal grid, analyze screen.

Blockage remains, perhaps
Pollen molecules or the nature of light
Itself. Run numbers find speed

Of wave propagation, trace photon
Zoom into eye. Reassemble
Synapse tree of steady waving

In brain. *Hello?* Nothing.
Maybe here to taunt, or instruct? Or: leaves
In wind? Higgs boson? Wings?

Definitely alive says evidence.
But biology's much harder than rocks.
Going to take time, eons. All

The time we have? Think,
Farm data, write: words & code.
Open screen, go outside. Breathe it in.

The Channel Swimmer

I know someone entering non-being in the worst way
With lesions & tumors & denial & that pain unknowable
Until you know. But the channel between fast-forward dying
& the rest of us—you can't swim it this time of year

Or anytime, until it's your turn & you get greased up
& spit in your goggles & ease your body into the wet shock
& push off, your love following in a rowboat beside,
Rowing through the grief chop & handing you energy bars

& attaboys. And you think wrong thoughts but don't say
Them, like, *Is that the best you can do, love, really?*
You, the one not *dying? Can't you join me, or at least*
Take turns being *me? Just a fucking energy bar, really?*

It's unfair, & the rest of us stand like lawn ornaments
Back on shore, one arm up & waving. Then slip
Into our cars & drive home because, well—what else
Can we do? No one we know has seen that other coast.

Epistemology

A man finds pieces he can reassemble,
A star space once here now dark and over there.
In the bath, an equation rises to the surface.
Another man finds a neck in the garrote
His hands make, cords and conduits pulsing.
This mind, this suspension of blood and water.
This concrete floor covered with sawdust.

All My Fathers

When they gathered to fete my passing
It was fall, the proper season for elegy, trees
Stripped to black & white. I offered
Drinks & some said *coffee*, others *juice,* or *water*.
A few wanted *whiskey*, which I did not have.

Many fathers filled the room, leaning
In close to one another, whispery abraded voices
So long unused the sound was strange
To them, & me. I recognized the heavy-lidded
English eyes from family daguerreotypes,

The near transparent German blues;
The freckled Scandinavian forearms, the sidelong
Irish grins. But when, I wondered,
Would the lesson start? There were windows
In place of every wall & an evening light

Leveled through the glass. Trees moved
Closer as one looked away, then quickly
Back. Or so it seemed. The fathers went on drinking.
And telling jokes, maybe—my ears were failing—
Voices reached me as if under water.

Then one father rose & tapped his glass—
The father closest to me, my own real father,
A forties-guy in a white t-shirt,
Arms muscled by hard labor. I tried reading
His lips but they were thin, & my eyes

Weak in the dimming light. I did notice
Nods all around reflecting father's speech

& was proud. Then, all began to fade
Into the gun-oil scented air of autumn. *That's
Your *stag*, daddy whispered. *Take the shot.*

White Boys from Hell

I did begin in the humid accented hell of Long Island
I did lick salt from the ceiling of hell
I did drag friends and family to hell and back, some I left
I did cough blood on their hell faces
I did sing hell to get laid
I did decompose years in the dim-lit old man bar of hell
I did punch holes in the wall to see hell unimpeded
I did invent a torture porn hell
I did snort cocaine from hell's breast and thigh and pubis
I did bring hell with me to the stock exchange floor
I did bring hell burning beneath my clothes
I did bring hell to marriage
I did cut chunks of hell-meat to roast over white coals
I did put my thumb on entire continents for the sheer hell of it
I did make movies of hell to run backwards
I did crawl out of hell bleeding
I did drag my body across the surface of the sun
I did leave a good part of me in hell
I did understand: I chose
I chose hell   I am free   I can go back

C&R PRESS CHAPBOOKS

C&R Press hosts two chapbook selection periods from June to September and November to March coupled with a reading in New York City each year. The Winter Soup Bowl and Summer Tide Pool Chapbook Series are open to new and established writers in poetry, fiction, essay and other creative writing.

2018 Winter Soup Bowl
Paleotemptestology by Bertha Crombet
White Boys from Hell by Jeffrey Skinner

2017 Summer Tide Pool
Atypical Cells of Undetermined Significance by Brenna Womer

2017 Winter Soup Bowl
Heredity and Other Inventions by Sharona Muir
On Inaccuracy by Joe Manning

2016 Summer Tide Pool
Cuntstruck by Kate Northrop
Relief Map by Erin M. Bertram
Love Undefined by Jonathan Katz

2016 Winter Soup Bowl
Notes from the Negro Side of the Moon by Earl Braggs
A Hunger Called Music: A Verse History in Black Music
by Meredith Nnoka

C&R PRESS TITLES

NONFICTION

Women in the Literary Landscape by Doris Weatherford, et al
Credo: An Anthology of Manifestos & Sourcebook for Creative
Writing by Rita Banerjee and Diana Norma Szokolyai

FICTION

Made by Mary by Laura Catherine Brown
Ivy vs. Dogg by Brian Leung
While You Were Gone by Sybil Baker
Cloud Diary by Steve Mitchell
Spectrum by Martin Ott
That Man in Our Lives by Xu Xi

SHORT FICTION

Notes From the Mother Tongue by An Tran
The Protester Has Been Released by Janet Sarbanes

ESSAY AND CREATIVE NONFICTION

Immigration Essays by Sybil Baker
Je suis l'autre: Essays and Interrogations by Kristina Marie Darling
Death of Art by Chris Campanioni

POETRY

My Stunt Double by Travis Denton
Lessons in Camoflauge by Martin Ott
Dark Horse by Kristina Marie Darling
All My Heroes are Broke by Ariel Francisco
Holdfast by Christian Anton Gerard
Ex Domestica by E.G. Cunningham
Like Lesser Gods by Bruce McEver
Notes from the Negro Side of the Moon by Earl Braggs
Imagine Not Drowning by Kelli Allen
Notes to the Beloved by Michelle Bitting
Free Boat: Collected Lies and Love Poems by John Reed
Les Fauves by Barbara Crooker
Tall as You are Tall Between Them by Annie Christain
The Couple Who Fell to Earth by Michelle Bitting
Notes to the Beloved by Michelle Bitting

www.ingramcontent.com/pod-product-compliance
Lightning Source LLC
Chambersburg PA
CBHW032110040426
42449CB00007B/1239